25 Money-Making Businesses

YOU CAN START IN YOUR SPARE TIME

Nevin M. Buconjic, MBA

Digital Adventures
Sault Ste. Marie, Ontario

Copyright © 2015 by Nevin M. Buconjic.

All rights reserved. No part of this publication may be reproduced, distributed or transmitted in any form or by any means, including photocopying, recording, or other electronic or mechanical methods, without the prior written permission of the publisher, except in the case of brief quotations embodied in critical reviews and certain other noncommercial uses permitted by copyright law. For permission requests, write to the publisher, addressed "Attention: Permissions Coordinator," at the address below.

Digital Adventures
130 Driftwood Drive
Echo Bay, Ontario, Canada
P0S 1C0
www.digitaladventures.ca

Book Layout ©2014 BookDesignTemplates.com

Ordering Information:
Quantity sales. Special discounts are available on quantity purchases by corporations, associations, and others. For details, contact the "Special Sales Department" at the address above or email: info@digitaladventures.ca

25 Money-Making Businesses You Can Start in Your Spare Time
Nevin M. Buconjic. — 4th Edition
ISBN-13: 978-1495373862
ISBN-10: 149537386X

Contents

About The Author 5

Thank You – Your FREE Bonus 7

About This Book 9

Introduction 11

Web Design Business 13

Photography Business 19

Tutoring Service 23

Virtual Assistant 25

Summer Day Camp 29

Computer Training Business 33

Graphic Design Business 37

T-shirt Design/Clothing Business 39

Freelance Writing 43

Party/Event Planner 47

Daycare Business 49

Mobile App/Software Developer 51

Business Planning and Consulting 55

Video Game Design 59

Crafts Business 63

Cake or Cupcake Business 65

Online Magazine or Blog 67

Internet/Social Media Marketing 71

House Cleaning Business 75

Gift Basket Business 77

Affiliate Marketing 79

Internet Retailer 83

Selling Online With Amazon FBA 87

EBook/Info-Product Author 93

Video Production 99

Conclusion 103

Resources & Information 105

    Other Books by Nevin M. Buconjic 107

To my wife Kristy and daughter Hannah.

About The Author

Nevin M. Buconjic is a serial entrepreneur, author, consultant and business analyst. Nevin holds degrees in marketing, computer science and an MBA, and has taught computers and business at the college and university level.

Nevin is the Founder of Startup Sault Ste. Marie (part of the Startup Canada network) and has founded and built multiple businesses including Digital Adventures, Interactive Minds Inc., Everyday Smart Living and StartUP Gear.

Nevin has mentored and counseled hundreds of small businesses, entrepreneurs and students.

In his spare time he enjoys spending time with his family, writing about business and technology, growing his various businesses and exploring online business opportunities.

Connect with Nevin online: www.nevinbuconjic.com
Facebook: www.facebook.com/NevinBuconjic
Twitter: www.twitter.com/nevinbuconjic
Amazon.com page: www.amazon.com/author/nevinbuconjic

Thank You – Your FREE Bonus

Thank you for buying *25 Money-Making Businesses You Can Start in Your Spare Time.*

I hope that you enjoy reading this book, and find the information to be valuable and helpful in your pursuit of a new chapter in your life.

As a special gift, be sure to grab a free copy of *Successful Entrepreneurs: What Makes Them Tick?*

Nevin

FREE BONUS - To download your FREE bonus report, visit: www.nevinbuconjic.com/entrepreneur_casestudy

In this report you will learn:

- How entrepreneurs seize opportunities to be successful…
- How to use technology to build your business…
- How to find a business that can be scaled up…
- 9 simple secrets to building a thriving business.

About This Book

This book is for anyone looking to create and take control of their own future. Whether you are graduating from college, have lost your job, or are just looking to make extra income, you will find plenty of ideas for your own business using the information found in this book.

Throughout the book I will provide examples of businesses which can be started either full-time or part-time, at a low cost or modest investment, and have the potential to be make significant profits!

The idea is the first step to business success. From there you can investigate the potential for making a profit, and determine if it is a good fit for you.

The number of resources, funding opportunities (grants and loans) and support available today for new entrepreneurs is unprecedented, and I will share links to valuable resources throughout the book.

You are not in this alone – so don't get discouraged before you even begin!

I have no doubt you will find at least one of the examples to be an option for starting your own business, and I also think that reading about 25 realistic businesses will spur you to think of many great ideas on your own.

Either way, this book is a great first step, and I hope it inspires you to take some chances and explore the world of entrepreneurship.

NOTE: Throughout this book you will find links to services I have used, more information on each particular business idea, and other small business resources. For your convenience, I have made all of the links available on my website for easy access. Please visit the webpage below to access all of the links.

Visit www.nevinbuconjic.com/25MoneyMakingBusinesses

Introduction

When I wrote the first edition of this book, America and the world were struggling through one of the most financially difficult periods in our lifetime. Economies had been turned upside down, and entire countries were going bankrupt. Millions of people had lost their homes, their jobs and their entire savings. I advised you to consider starting a business in order to create your own opportunities, develop skills and earn extra income.

As I write this fourth edition, the tide is turning and prospects have improved, along with economic growth.

In this prosperous environment where employment is on the rise, economies are looking better, and new money is being pumped into markets, I urge you to consider starting your own business so you can carve out a piece of this incredible opportunity!

There is no better time to chart your own path, and rely on your own skills and ideas to create your own success. Whether you start a part-time business for extra income, or jump right into a full-time venture, starting your own business can be a very rewarding and prosperous experience.

In order to give you the best chance for success, I am going to coach you on having the right mindset to successfully start and grow your own small business.

This book will provide you with the foundation you need to get started, and it will point you in the direction of other small business resources available to help ensure your continued success.

Coming up with a great business idea can be tough. There are lots of ways to explore your talents, skills or interests for business ideas – this is a good place to start.

Business opportunities can be hiding in plain sight, literally right in front of your nose, and with the examples I'll give you, you're going to be able to see them when nobody else does!

Within this book are 25 ideas for businesses you can start today. Many of these business ideas are from my own experience working with entrepreneurs. They have done it and so can you.

So what are you waiting for – this could be the start of a brand new chapter in your life – one where you are in control of your own future.

Good luck in your journey.

CHAPTER 1

Web Design Business

While designing your own website is easier today than ever before, businesses still require talented designers to build attractive, user-friendly websites to promote their business and even sell online. If you have the skills necessary (think HTML, Photoshop, JavaScript, and other programming languages) to build a web site from scratch, or experience building sites using WordPress and other platforms, then you can turn those skills into a profitable business! Through my experience, a lot of young people are attracted to this idea as it is a fairly inexpensive business to start.

Typical expenses to start a web design business would include a PC/MAC or laptop (which you probably already own), web design software (eg. Dreamweaver, Photoshop and other graphics programs ~ $200-1,000) and a decent digital camera, which would cost $200-500.

Many designers create websites from scratch, but this requires significant design skills. If you aren't a graphic designer and can't afford to hire one just yet, an alternative is to purchase website templates which are both affordable ($50-100 each) and very professional looking. You can check out www.templatemonster.com to see what I mean.

These web templates are fully customizable, and easy to use. There is a wide selection available to meet almost any category, almost guaranteeing that you will find one that fits your client's needs.

Another option is to utilize WordPress. WordPress is a blogging platform upon which you can install themes; to customize your sites, as well as plug-ins to add functionality. WordPress is easy to use and very powerful. I now rely solely on WordPress for all of my websites. I just purchase and install a theme and then customize it according to my needs. I regularly use www.studiopress.com for high quality themes, but there are many other options as well.

In terms of getting started, it may be easiest to tackle a local market first – local small businesses and not-for-profit organizations make excellent customers. Once you prove yourself, and are able to build a portfolio, you can expand your business - finding clients online. The beauty of a web design business is that through online communication and file sharing, you can build sites for clients almost anywhere in the world and never even have to meet the client face-to-face.

Through my experience, I have found that there are often several high-end web design companies in a particular city or area, servicing major companies, and charging significant fees. These companies can't be bothered with the smaller design jobs and small budgets - which opens up a market for your business!

Make sure to price your services for the market you are serving. What do your competitors charge? Because a business' website is so important, most businesses will not hesitate to spend a few thousand dollars for a quality site that reflects their brand and meets their needs.

In many cases, I have seen web design companies promoting websites for $200-500. Cheaper is not always better, and in most cases, the clients get what they pay for. Low prices might get you some clients, but a low cost strategy isn't typically the best strategy. In fact, at those prices it would be difficult to make a profit – don't forget your time is valuable – make sure you are recouping a decent wage for each project.

A common mistake many small businesses make is to undervalue the true cost of their services. Charging by the hour may be appropriate for some services, but often times charging by the job or project is more appropriate. A good rule of thumb is that a project will always take longer than we estimate - so consider building in a buffer.

Most web designers provide a complete quote or proposal based on the scope of the project (design, number of pages, features, functionality) as opposed to a fixed price.

If you are serious about starting a web design business, then the first step is to determine your skill level and what software you will have available. I recommend purchasing a few books on web design, HTML 5 and even a book on the specific software program you will use (Dreamweaver for example). Alternatively you could search for tutorials and examples online...trust me, there is plenty of free info online.

There are also numerous online services that allow you to build websites without programming or design experience (eg. www.wix.com). While the end result can be an attractive site, your clients will most likely expect you to build their site using your web design skills.

Start building websites! Build a site for your business, which you can use to promote your business, and as part of your portfolio - which clients will want to see. Try to build at least 2-3 sites for your portfolio before searching out additional clients.

Finally, seek out businesses or organizations in your area which do not have a website or have one that looks outdated or unprofessional. Contact the organization and tell them what you can do for them. Be prepared to show them your portfolio and past work.

Another strategy, which was used heavily by a local firm I competed against, was to create a mock-up for the proposed site and show it to the client. If the client is impressed or excited by the design, there is a good chance they will want to engage your services.

With web design, the work often speaks for itself. If you create attractive and user-friendly websites for your clients, then it will be much easier to find new clients.

For more information, tips and ideas visit these websites:

http://freelanceswitch.com/freelance-web-development/start-web-design-business
http://under30ceo.com/15-reasons-to-start-a-web-development-business
www.godaddy.com
http://wordpress.org

CHAPTER 2

Photography Business

Photography is a great business for creative people. It is something that takes skill and experience, but can definitely be learned. With a modest investment in a good DSLR camera, a few different lenses, and some lighting/flash equipment ($500-3,000) you will be ready for business.

It is a good idea to read as many books and magazines on photography as you can to learn the ins-and-outs of taking different types of pictures and the camera settings that will be needed to achieve the best possible shots. And of course get out there and practice!

The main clients/jobs for this type of business will include family portraits, weddings, baby portraits, and possibly even news coverage (freelance work). Because the majority of the jobs you book will be very important events for the clients, you must ensure that you have the necessary skills and practice to deliver great work. The last thing you want is for the client to be unhappy with the shots - imagine the devastation if a newlywed couple's wedding photos did not turn out well!

Good photographers can be hard to find, and word-of-mouth will spread quickly if you do a great job (and maybe more quickly if you don't). I know several people who have started out part-time and then quit their full-time jobs because their businesses have grown so fast. This is one business where talent and creativity will pay dividends!

One of the things that sets photographers apart from each other is the use of creativity in their shots. Don't be afraid to step out of the box. One entrepreneurial photographer I know has made a name for himself because he takes a lot of non-traditional photos - and the result is fun, exciting and cool looking pictures. Because of his interesting - or you could say unique - style, his business has grown tremendously as a result of word-of-mouth and social media.

This individual posts preview shots on his blog, and shares them through social media like Facebook and Twitter, garnering a lot of comments and views along the way.

Having the photography skills is one aspect of the business, but as mentioned above, it will be important to promote and showcase your work in order to build your client base. At the bare minimum you should have a blog or website where you can post your work, along with information about your style or techniques, pricing and available packages. Provide contact information and encourage clients to contact you as soon as possible to book dates.

Most photographers ask for a deposit up front in order to reserve a date. This is a good practice, because you don't want to turn down a job because you are already booked, only to have the existing client cancel. Requiring a deposit usually ensures that only serious clients book your time.

Visit these websites for more information, tips and ideas:

http://virtualphotographystudio.com/photographyblog
http://currentphotographer.com/from-conception-to-birth-a-business-is-born

CHAPTER 3

Tutoring Service

Are you really good in a particular school subject? Does math, physics or history come naturally to you? If so, you could be an excellent tutor for hire. Whether it is at the elementary, high school or college level - there are usually plenty of students in need of some extra help in school. And the best part is, it will only cost you your time.

A tutoring business can be set up at a very low cost - mainly just your time and marketing costs. Advertise through local classified ads, internet postings, and flyers at schools, local grocery stores and coffee shops. You can usually sign up directly with a university or college (and possibly your local public school board) to provide these private services as well.

Develop your own website to promote your services and allow parents and students to contact you directly. Set up social media accounts and offer valuable information to prospective clients and followers. Social media is an excellent tool for promoting your business, and building your brand as an excellent choice for tutoring services.

If you are a student yourself, this can provide great experience for your college application, or as a stepping stone to your future teaching career. Not to mention the extra cash you will make on the side.

Startup costs for a tutoring service are typically limited to marketing and promotion, but could include supplies and/or particular software - depending on the subjects you focus on. A laptop would be useful for running the business, and there may be software available which you could use directly with students. Transportation costs should also be factored in as tutoring would most likely occur at the client's home or school.

There are franchises for this type of service in many communities, such as Scholars. Make sure to check and see if there is any direct competition in your area. Most of the franchises require parents to pay for blocks of services (eg. six sessions) which can add up in cost. You may benefit by offering lower prices, and more convenience - with no minimum number of sessions.

Visit these websites for more information, tips and ideas:

www.americantutoringassociation.org/index.php
www.tutoring-expert.com/starting-a-tutoring-business.html
www.thetutoringbusiness.com/tutoringbusiness.html
www.thetutoringbusiness.com/tutoringbusinessstartups.html

CHAPTER FOUR

Virtual Assistant

A virtual assistant (VA) is an independent contractor who provides administrative, technical or creative services remotely. VA's are usually hired by businesses and professionals in need of help or particular skills. Communication is typically via email, online chatting or the telephone.

Utilizing VA's can save businesses considerable expense such as office space, equipment costs, vacation and benefit costs, etc. which is helping to fuel the growth of this industry. Additionally, employers are billed only for the work that is completed, making VA's a very affordable alternative to additional employees.

The VA provides value by allowing companies to focus on the important aspects of their business, while delegating particular assignments and projects to the VA.

Becoming a virtual assistant might be the perfect fit for individuals with administrative experience, skills such as graphic design, web development, research, writing and communications skills. You can work with clients from around the world, in the comfort of your own home.

As a virtual assistant, you have the ability to choose the type of work you are most interested in. When promoting your services, you can highlight specific specialties and experiences that may qualify you for work that other's might not, but most VA's will typically provide a base level of administrative services as well.

Many virtual assistants I have come across offer general administrative as well as specialized skills such as eBook formatting or cover design. The ability to offer specialized skills can set you apart or allow you to focus on a niche market.

A recent article on Entrepreneur.com listed 10 popular tasks for outsourcing to virtual assistants: bookkeeping, online research, database entry, data presentations, managing email, social tasks, travel research, scheduling, chasing business and industry knowledge prep. You can read the article by visiting the following link: www.entrepreneur.com/article/225318

As with any profession, experience requirements in this industry vary, but most VA's have several years of experience in their particular specialty.

Finding work as a virtual assistant can be achieved through the use of websites such as oDesk.com and elance.com which match candidates and employers. You can create a profile listing your skills, experience and required wages, and employers can contact you directly. These sites also track the number of jobs you have completed and provide additional benefits for businesses, to make the process easier and reliable.

Many virtual assistants also have their own websites and promote their services using social media and other web marketing. Wages typically range from $5 - $50 per hour, depending on the level of skill and experience as well as location of the individual.

There are numerous websites and associations which provide more detail about becoming a virtual assistant as well as offering training programs.

To read about one busy executive's experience using a virtual assistant, visit the link: http://michaelhyatt.com/my-experience-using-a-virtual-assistant.html

For more information, visit these websites:

www.oDesk.com - Top 10 Virtual Assistant Contractors
Canadian Virtual Assistant Connection - www.cvac.ca
Canadian Virtual Assistant Network - www.canadianva.net
International Virtual Assistants Association - www.ivaa.org
www.entrepreneur.com/article/71516

CHAPTER 5

Summer Day Camp

Every community needs summer camps for kids. But they don't have to be the camping in the woods type, or even an overnight camp. Day camps are extremely popular, and give parents options to keep their kids learning, and entertained. Day camps could include sports camps, computers, photography, acting and theatre camp, science camp...there are so many possibilities. Your own skills, talents and knowledge will dictate what topics you focus on.

The important thing with a summer camp is to fill a niche that is not being met. Do a web search to see what is already being offered in your community and what opportunities may exist (also check out your local YMCA, colleges and universities - chances are they offer summer camps).

I started a computer camp for kids in my own community. I rented space at a local university, which gave us the location and equipment, as well as a fun learning environment. This also gave us instant credibility.

The close links to the university helped us to establish a strong footprint in the community, and helped the camps to grow significantly over the years. The university was very supportive, and welcomed the opportunity to have more young people on campus.

The startup costs for a summer camp can be significant depending on what kind of equipment or space is needed. In my case, I needed software licenses, paid rent for the use of the university computer lab, had employees to pay and marketing costs ranged from $1,500 - 3,000 per year. Because I was also teaching the camps when I started, I was able to keep costs fairly low the first year.

I grew the business gradually and did not require any financing to start (other than a credit card). It was a very successful and rewarding experience. Marketing was done on the cheap using inexpensive flyers (distributed for free within the school system), Internet and social media marketing (our website was the hub), our email list and through limited newspaper advertising. After 10 years, I sold the business to a former "computer camper" and assistant instructor of the camps!

In order to offer a summer camp, you need to create lessons, schedules and other components of daily activity. In my case, we developed computer-based lessons in web design, video game design and more. We made sure each day had a mix of lessons/presentations, videos, outdoor activity and free time to work on projects. Because significant time was spent on computers, it was important to parents that their children spent some time outside and away from the lab.

Every camp will be different and depending on the topic - computers, sports, art etc. you will need to develop the appropriate mix of learning time, fun time, social time and free time.

I will leave you with some thoughts on competition. When considering competition, look at all kids camps available, not just comparing computer camps for example. One lesson I quickly learned was that many parents need summer activities for their children, and therefore send them to multiple camps over the summer. In some cases, you are simply a babysitting alternative.

My point is that you are competing with every other camp available, so it's important not to price your camps out of the ball park. Be conscious of the prices of other camps, but don't forgo profits either.

In my local market I found that $200 per week for day camps was about the limit the market would bear. I would have loved to have charged double or triple that like I have seen elsewhere, but it just wasn't feasible.

Visit these websites for more information, tips and ideas:

http://www.ourkids.net/
http://www.businessweek.com/articles/2012-05-01/mapping-the-summer-camp-business
http://www.wisebread.com/summer-camp-as-a-side-business

CHAPTER SIX

Computer Training Business

Do your friends, family and even co-workers come to you with their computer problems? Are you regularly asked to fix their computer or show them how to use particular software? Why not make money from your computer skills?

Significant opportunities exist for computer training businesses. As computer and Internet developments continue at a rapid pace, more and more of the older generation is being left behind. But these people want to learn to use computers so they can communicate with their grandchildren, download their photos from a digital camera, or even learn to use email and surf the Internet! You would be surprised at the things that come so naturally for you, but are difficult for older people to comprehend.

If you are excellent with computers and other technology, and possess good people skills, you might consider starting a business that delivers these services.

You can provide private learning sessions, tech support or rent space at a local college computer lab and teach full classes. Early on in my business, I did just that. I put together a basic computing course for adults - to learn to use email, the Internet, and Microsoft Office basics. Amazingly it sold out the first time! It was a great experience, and highly profitable. The only reason I did not continue offering classes for adults was the time commitment. I was too busy with web design clients, and my computer camps program. But this could be an excellent opportunity in your community.

The costs of running such a business are minimal as you will be teaching the client how to use their own equipment! If you will be offering classes then the costs will include rental fees, advertising and more.

For private lessons you could charge by the hour, and promote your business through inexpensive classified ads, by placing flyers on supermarket bulletin boards (and other locations) and even by targeting your neighborhood with flyers. This is also the type of business that can grow quickly due to positive word-of-mouth, so make sure to have business cards to hand out and give a few extra to your clients - they will be happy to recommend you!

Of course having a website or blog will be a good idea - you do want to showcase your skills after all. And if anyone uses a search engine to find computer training locally, you want to make sure your website is on the first page of the results.

By utilizing social media, you can continually offer your clients and followers tips and advice as well as links to interesting articles. They will appreciate it, and maybe they will want to learn more about those topics!

Visit these websites for more information, tips and ideas:

www.morebusiness.com/computer-training-business
http://sbinformation.about.com/od/business-ideas/qt/Computer-Training-Small-Business-Idea.htm

CHAPTER SEVEN

Graphic Design Business

Graphic design is a growing field because so many small businesses require skilled designers to produce marketing materials and collateral. This an excellent freelance business where you can work from home and deliver your finished products either digitally or have the finished product printed locally without the need to invest in expensive equipment.

Typical products and services would include the design and printing of business cards, flyers, brochures, newsletters, designing logos and even signs. Graphic design is integral to the web design process as well, which might provide opportunities to partner with other companies to deliver full services.

Standard equipment would include a PC/MAC, a printer, desk, and chair. Special high-end software may be required such as Adobe Photoshop and Illustrator for example, which can be expensive. However, often student editions of the same software is available (if you qualify) for a fraction of the price or freeware programs like Google Docs, GIMP and more.

Most graphic designers attend college to learn their trade and gain valuable experience; however, many are also naturally talented or self-taught. Do you have the skills and talent to pursue this type of work?

You can build your business by focusing on local clients, as well as utilizing websites such as www.elance.com to bid on design jobs. Graphic designers can make very good wages as fees charged can be significant.

Visit these websites for more information, tips and ideas:

www.graphicartistsguild.org
www.graphicdesignblender.com/starting-your-own-design-business

CHAPTER EIGHT

T-shirt Design/Clothing Business

If you are an artistic or creative individual, you might consider a custom t-shirt or clothing company. Depending on your level of skill, you can design the clothing and outsource the production (locally or online), but for even greater profits, consider purchasing the equipment and doing it yourself.

I remember working with one individual who was able to buy an older style manual screen printing machine for less than $100, and I've seen starter kits for $199 online. He started producing t-shirts with his own unique designs, and was quite successful in a summer entrepreneurship program I was involved in.

Before investing in equipment, you may wish to try out your designs first to see if they catch on. Original graphic designs, images or even slogans can be quite popular - but be careful not to use trademarked material. You can find plenty of t-shirts with "unauthorized" logos and imagery on places like eBay - but do this at your own risk, as the copyright or trademark holder could take legal action against you. This is obviously not recommended.

Your merchandise could be sold at local clothing stores, flea markets and more. Depending on your target market, there could be other outlets for your designs such as skateboard or sporting goods stores. You never know, your designs could be a huge hit!

Plain t-shirts and other supplies can be acquired online in bulk. Add your designs and significantly mark up the cost to earn a nice profit.

Another way to profit from t-shirt and clothing designs is to utilize online services such as www.teespring.com. These services allow you to create campaigns to sell your unique designs at no cost to you. Simply set sales targets to determine your profit levels – if your campaign sells the required volume of t-shirts, then the shirts are printed and orders fulfilled - and you get paid. If the campaign does not sell the volume required, then customers are notified that the orders will not be completed.

T-shirt campaigns can be quite successful, and there is no risk to you. Of course you may incur expenses promoting the offers.

Popular marketing platforms for t-shirt campaigns include Facebook, Twitter and other social media, as well as promoting on your own website or email list.

Visit these websites for more information, tips and ideas:

www.1stwebdesigner.com/inspiration/superb-t-shirt-designs
http://naldzgraphics.net/tutorials/30-outstanding-t-shirt-designs-tutorials-and-tips
www.threadless.com/submissions

CHAPTER NINE

Freelance Writing

If you are a gifted writer, with the skills to write different kinds of content, then a freelance writing business could be a good fit for you. Everything from news articles and product reviews on websites and blogs, to marketing materials for small businesses could be possible.

Are there local publications or news websites in your area? These could be potential clients for your business - since they are in the business of providing information and content to their subscribers.

Consider reaching out to your local college/university that publishes an alumni magazine, or offer to write a column for a local free newspaper.

Put together a portfolio of your writing samples or start your own blog to showcase your work, then contact these companies. Try pitching specific ideas for articles and then direct them to your samples for further evidence of your writing abilities.

Typically all that is needed for this type of business is a computer or tablet, with printer and Internet access, and word processor software. If you will be doing interviews you may wish to purchase a small tape recorder, or even use your smartphone - most iPhone or Android devices have voice recording apps.

Marketing this type of service will be very targeted - send writing samples along with your story ideas directly to the editors of blogs, websites or newspapers. Offer to guest post on a popular blog to increase your exposure and deliver some traffic back to your own website.

Don't be afraid to volunteer your services for free in order to build your portfolio.

Your website or blog should have all of your writing samples, as well as content to demonstrate your expertise. Build your social media presence so that you can share your work and drive traffic.

Research local businesses to determine if they typically produce newsletters, web content or even annual reports. Contact these companies to offer your services.

Many businesses and organizations find it challenging to dedicate the time to develop new information, customer stories or content for their websites - they might just be looking for someone with your skills!

Freelance writing can be a very rewarding business. You will be involved in a variety of projects and write about a great variety of topics. You may also choose to focus on particular niche areas - such as corporate communications or the fitness industry if that is where your interest or experience lies.

Visit these websites for more information, tips and ideas:

http://homepreneurs.net/2012/01/31/start-a-home-based-freelance-writing-business
http://sbinformation.about.com/od/business-ideas/qt/Freelance-Writing-Small-Business-Idea.htm
http://freelancefolder.com
http://writing-journey.com/how-to-make-money-from-your-writing-online/how-to-start-your-freelance-writing-business-building-your-portfolio

CHAPTER TEN

Party/Event Planner

Are you socially connected or the life of the party? Do your friends look to you to see what is going on every weekend? Do you have experience planning and throwing parties and events? Why not make money by planning other people's parties and events?

In today's fast-paced world, people either don't have the time or the patience to organize their own events - or they are simply overwhelmed by the experience. They need the assistance of a professional!

Good communication skills and organizational skills are essential to party and event planning. You could be responsible for coordinating anything from weddings and birthday parties, to charity and business events. Attention to detail is key, as you may be required to handle everything from sending invitations, to arranging for food catering and decorating the venue.

But the reward is a successful event, a happy client and referrals for even more work.

Startup requirements may include a laptop computer, cell phone, and access to regular transportation. Through experience, you will develop a solid list of contacts for catering, music, decorations etc. but this might require research and pounding the payment in the beginning.

Word-of-mouth is one way to build this type of business, especially when guests at your events see such wonderful work. It is still advisable to have a website where you can list clients, and show photos of your best events. Potential clients can get an idea of your style and skills by checking out your past work.

To download an excellent free guide on event planning, visit: www.bizymoms.com/cart/careers/e-books/event_planner_ebook.pdf

Visit these websites for more information, tips and ideas:

www.entrepreneur.com/article/37892
www.fabjob.com/partyplanner.asp

CHAPTER ELEVEN

Daycare Business

Do you enjoy working with children? Do you have experience raising your own children or babysitting multiple children? In many families these days, it is common for both parents to work and have careers. These families often need reliable childcare at reasonable prices.

You may have an opportunity to provide child care for multiple clients, or there may be an opportunity to care for multiple children at once. Many jurisdictions allow for the care of up to four children (in addition to your own) before any sort of licensing is required (check with your state/provincial and municipal regulations).

Consider opening a daycare in your home. You may wish to use dedicated space in your home, but most likely the children will use common areas of your home; therefore, make sure to discuss the opportunity with your family first.

Depending on the ages of the children, you can assemble a number of toys, children's books and activities and earn four times the money in the same amount of time! Of course, you would be responsible for things like food and drinks, and costs for crafts, diapers and any other materials.

The daycare business can provide fantastic write-offs at tax time. Don't forget to calculate the portion of your home utilized by the daycare as you can typically write-off a proportion of home expenses such as your cable TV, electricity and heating, Internet, and any supplies, food etc. used by the business.

Marketing could involve letting your neighbors know about your daycare service (hopefully they will tell their friends), posting flyers around the neighborhood, or even placing classified ads in the newspaper or online. Many clients are obtained through word-of-mouth.

Before pursuing such an opportunity, make sure you have taken qualified child care and first-aid courses, and have proper experience (including raising your own children). Child care is a great responsibility and you want to show your clients that you are qualified to take care of their children.

Visit these websites for more information, tips and ideas:

www.entrepreneur.com/article/41422
www.canadabusiness.ab.ca/index.php/start-up/33-starting-a-childcare-centre
www.sba.gov/community/blogs/community-blogs/small-business-matters/starting-child-care-business-government-tools

CHAPTER TWELVE

Mobile App/Software Developer

Creating mobile apps has become big business. With marketplaces such Apple's iTunes App Store, BlackBerry World and the various Android marketplaces, there is the opportunity to sell to hundreds of millions of smartphone and tablet users around the globe.

There are hundreds, if not thousands of examples of programmers and companies making a lot of money selling their apps - even at just $0.99 each! All it takes is a good idea for an app or mobile game.

While the competition can be stiff - Apple iTunes for example has over a million different apps available - it is still considered by some to be the "Gold Rush" of the 21st century. The opportunity to make money selling apps is huge, because the number of potential customers is so large and the app marketplaces make it so easy to find your apps.

If you already have programming skills and are curious about what it takes to make apps for Apple iOS or Android or BlackBerry, I recommend you do a web search on the subject. There are plenty of tutorials and information online, as well as developer manuals.

For more in-depth material, you may wish to purchase one or two books on the subject. Next you will want to start practicing and see what you can come up with. In most cases, all you need is your computer.

There is even software available that allows you to build apps and games with no programming necessary. I recommend you check out www.gameacademy.com for software and training on starting your own app business, and www.appgamekit.com to learn about the App Game Kit.

Additionally, all of the smartphone companies have developer kits which typically include software you can use to do the programming, and then test the app using simulator software. Some of these developer kits cost money - so be sure to visit their websites for more information:

- Apple iOS Dev Center
- BlackBerry Developer
- Android Developer Kit
- Microsoft Windows Phone - App Hub

There are numerous ways to make money with apps. Many app companies get started by releasing free apps, or apps supported by advertising. This can be a good business model for building awareness of your studio and your apps. Subsequent apps or even pro versions without advertising can be put up for sale as well.

For some ideas check out this article on TechRadar: www.techradar.com/news/software/applications/how-to-make-money-from-app-development-943970 .

For tips on making money with children's apps, visit: www.guardian.co.uk/technology/appsblog/2013/mar/21/indie-developers-apps-for-kids

There is no guarantee you will get rich in the smartphone app market, but it is possible. There are even examples of 10-12 year old kids building successful apps.

Visit these websites for more information, tips and ideas:

www.entrepreneur.com/article/223177
http://mashable.com/2012/05/01/start-an-app-business
www.instantappwizard.com/Mobile-Apps-Business.php
www.dummies.com/how-to/content/starting-an-iphone-application-business-for-dummie.html
www.inc.com/guides/2010/07/how-to-write-a-business-plan-for-a-mobile-gaming-company.html
www.bafta.org/games/game-features/creating-successful-apps,3212,BA.html

CHAPTER THIRTEEN

Business Planning and Consulting

Many business owners and potential entrepreneurs require a business plan in order to obtain funding or qualify for small business assistance. This may present an opportunity for you if you have the skills, experience or education required.

Are you a business student or do you have experience developing business plans or feasibility studies? Why not capitalize on your knowledge and experience by writing business plans and doing other consulting work for small business startups?

From my own experience, most small business help offices will provide clients with assistance to develop their plan - but they won't write it for them. While it is a good idea for the business owner to write the plan themselves, sometimes they just don't have the time or skills to do a good job.

This is where you come in. Utilizing your market research, financial skills and business knowledge, you could offer your services to these clients for a fee. In many cases, the small business help offices may promote your services for you.

You can often earn thousands of dollars per business plan. There are plenty of books on the subject; you may even have some already. Dust off your college business textbooks or more recent books on the subject and read about the components of a business plan to get started.

The business plan is meant to explain what the business is, how it will operate and how it will make money. Often-times, a business plan is required to obtain financing.

Typically, all you will need to carry this out is a computer, printer and perhaps business planning software - which you can purchase for less than $100. By using software, with built in templates and financial statements, you can simply fill in the blanks and customize each plan using the information and data specific to that business.

Market your business through existing small business help offices, economic development organizations, Chamber of Commerce newsletters and other forms of local advertising.

Create a website which can demonstrate your qualifications, and showcase samples you have created. Attend networking opportunities with local business groups to spread the word.

More recently, there has been a movement away from writing formal business plans, and moving towards the concept of lean startup, creating one-page business plans, or focusing on business models.

These new concepts present additional opportunities for you, as businesses and organizations are anxious to learn more about them. You could become experienced in these concepts and offer to guide clients through the process of implementing or creating them.

Visit these websites for more information, tips and ideas:

www.entrepreneur.com/article/41384
www.businessmodelgeneration.com/canvas/bmc
www.canadabusiness.ab.ca/index.php/start-up/35-starting-a-consulting-business
www.powerhomebiz.com/business-ideas/how-to-be-a-consultant.htm
www.canadabusiness.ca/eng/page/2753/
http://theleanstartup.com/
www.bplans.com

CHAPTER FOURTEEN

Video Game Design

Video game design has come a long way from the early days when one person could create their own successful game in their basement. Today's video game industry rivals that of the movie industry both in earnings, and development budgets. Successful video games cost millions of dollars and require teams of talented people to produce.

But there are still opportunities and markets for indie games, whether for the PC, game consoles or mobile devices. With just a few people (programmer, and graphic designer for example) you can still produce games which can sell - especially in the mobile space (Apple iOS, Android, BlackBerry).

When I started my computer camps program in 2001, the main focus was on teaching fun computing skills and web design - game design was just one day out of a week's camp. By the second year, game design had become its own week-long camp and by the next year dominated our camp offering – including 3D game design and FPS game design.

There is no doubt that the video game industry is huge and growing, and that teens and youth are interested in learning how to build their own games.

In my own community, the sector has become a focus of many educational institutions and organizations in order to grow a local high-tech gaming industry.

There are programs available for teens and young people which teach them the skills needed to succeed in this sector. If you are in high school or college, make sure to check your local area for training opportunities.

Creating video games requires skills in programming, computer graphics, 3D animation, and more. If you are a programmer, you might consider partnering with others who have the computer graphics and other skills you may need.

You will need the right equipment which would include a PC or MAC, necessary software and/or development kits, and perhaps the game consoles or mobile devices which you are designing for.

There are also excellent software programs which allow you to build games yourself quite easily – just bring your imagination!

Some of these programs I have personally used in my computer camps program, such as the Games Factory, FPS Creator,

3D Game Maker (check out www.thegamecreators.com for more information) and Microsoft XNA Game Studio.

Starting a video game design company is surely not the easiest business venture mentioned in this book. But if you have the skills and experience, it might be a great opportunity.

Visit these websites for more information, tips and ideas:

www.entrepreneur.com/blog/220506
http://makeitbigingames.com/2006/06/five-realistic-steps-to-starting-a-game-development-company
www.ehow.com/how_5082012_start-gaming-company.html
www.game-guru.com

CHAPTER FIFTEEN

Crafts Business

Are you artistic and enjoy making wonderful creations with your own hands and imagination? Starting a home-based crafts business could be the ultimate combination of your favorite hobby and making money.

You may already have a specialty - maybe you are into ceramics and pottery, soap making, or candle making.

Other ideas could include creating doll clothing, quilting, painting rocks and wood slices, or making wreaths. Holiday inspirations could lead to some really fun and timely crafts for Halloween, Easter, Thanksgiving and Christmas.

You might even consider jewelry design. Relying on your fashion sense and knowledge of what is trendy, you can capitalize on this by designing and producing your own style of jewelry! Most of the required components can be purchased at hobby supply or craft stores. Stones, beads, shells, sparkles or whatever design elements you choose can be made into unique creations.

Although the ideas can be endless, don't be afraid to specialize. You may be really talented at creating stained glass items, but only so-so at candle making. Figure out what you are good at, most creative with or best known for. Once you establish your product line, you may also decide to offer custom work - this can be very lucrative.

Don't be afraid to experiment and try new things, but focus on your specialties as well.

How will you sell your creations? Luckily, there are many options for selling including local flea markets, craft fairs, eBay, Etsy.com and other outlets.

Visit these websites for more information:

http://craftgossip.com
www.craftbits.com
www.countryliving.com/crafts/projects/craft-ideas
www.design-unique-handcrafted-jewelry.com
www.sheknows.com/living/home-crafts/articles
www.etsy.com
www.entrepreneur.com/article/76936

CHAPTER SIXTEEN

Cake or Cupcake Business

Do you love to bake? Are you creative and have the ability to make works of art in the kitchen? Want to start a fun and delicious home business? Custom cakes and cupcakes are big business. So big and popular, they have spawned their own television reality shows! But these yummy treats can no longer just taste great; they must look great too.

To be successful in this business is as much about design and artistic ability as it is about mixing the right ingredients. To excel and gain clients, you will need a portfolio to show off your best work. This might include examples of birthday cakes, other themed cakes and cupcakes. The perfect medium to showcase your work would be your own website or blog.

Make sure to list your contact information and any other relevant details about your business. Utilize Pinterest, Facebook and Twitter to promote your business and share pictures of your latest work.

It is important for your business to offer a regular menu of items, as well as specializing in particular flavors or kinds of cakes and cupcakes. Custom orders can also be profitable.

The largest cost in running this type of business is typically the cost of the ingredients themselves. If you are operating out of your home, you will already most likely have an oven, mixer, measuring cups and other necessary items. You may, however, need to purchase a number of cupcake or cake pans and other specialized tools.

Check to see if there is a wholesale restaurant supply store in your area or purchase bulk ingredients at Costco and other bulk food stores to cut down on costs.

Make sure to check local regulations for food preparation businesses. Your home may require a visit by a local health inspector. Check with your municipality for details.

There are a lot of cookbooks on making cakes and cupcakes. You can get plenty of ideas from these and monthly magazines as well. Check your local library, bookstore or Amazon.com to see what is available.

Visit these websites for more information, tips and ideas:

http://cupcake-business.com
www.ehow.com/how_6552215_open-cupcake-business.html
www.mainstreet.com/article/small-business/launching/small-biz-101-how-start-cupcake-shop

CHAPTER SEVENTEEN

Online Magazine or Blog

Quick, name your top three favorite blogs! Maybe you said TMZ for your celebrity fix, or TechCrunch for your tech news and the Huffington Post for your latest news. Blogs are hugely popular and have become legitimate news outlets. Readership is huge and advertising revenues can be even bigger.

If you are an expert on a particular topic or simply want to blog about your interests and knowledge, blogging can be a potential business and revenue stream.

Setting up a high-quality blogging site is easier than ever and there are lots of options for platforms including WordPress, Blogger and Tumblr. I have used both WordPress and Blogger, and my preference is for WordPress.

Your blog can be set up in a matter of hours. Then your content becomes the key. Check out www.studiopress.com for some great WordPress templates.

Blogging can involve writing about topics you are interested in, writing about experiences, and even doing product or book reviews - the possibilities are endless. But the writing should be high quality and the posts should be interesting. Remember, the idea is to build a readership of people with similar interests and eventually monetize the site with advertising and potentially affiliate links to products.

You can search the Internet for numerous tips on successful blogging, but it basically boils down to a few key points. You must post regularly - this could be daily or several times per week, but your readers will count on regular activity. This can be challenging and time consuming, so make sure you are up for the task, or there is little point in starting a blog.

High traffic is the key to getting advertising sponsors, and plenty of click-throughs on your syndicated ads (Google AdSense, Bing etc.). You must build your readership to make money with blogging.

Most successful blogs have teams of reporters and writers to add enough content, but it is still possible to have a successful blog even if you are the only contributor. This is especially true if you focus on niche areas and topics where you can be seen as an expert. Additionally, using guest bloggers and other techniques can help add to your regular content.

I started my first blog to showcase my growing number of technology articles and from there began to do product reviews. My reviews of several Blackberry smartphone products were noticed by Blackberry and I was invited to join their

Blackberry Elite program which provides early access to products, company initiatives and more. I attended the Blackberry 10 product launch in New York City in January 2013, all expenses paid! A nice perk for blogging!

I was getting traffic to the blog, utilizing Google AdSense, and had revenue coming in. But, I did not have the time to dedicate to running a successful blog and eventually shut it down. I tried many different things, and I look at those couple of years as an experiment. Now I blog and post my articles or short stories directly on my personal website, but I learned a lot from the experience of running my own blog.

Go back to your favorite blogs, and make note of the particular layout, ad placement and other factors. Now go to Google and look for blogs in your areas of interest. You will no doubt find a number of professional and personal blogs - both are valuable for getting ideas of how your own blog should look.

With the right effort, you can create a successful money-making blog. There are plenty of examples out there.

Visit these websites for more information, tips and ideas:

www.subhub.com/how-to-start-an-online-magazine
www.wow-womenonwriting.com/34-How2-StartEzine.html
http://thebacklight.com/have-a-successful-blog-1-3-hours-a-day
www.famousbloggers.net/building-successful-blog.html
www.adsense.com

CHAPTER EIGHTEEN

Internet/Social Media Marketing

You may have grown up with the Internet, and for you the use of social media is second nature. But many others struggle to use it for fun, let alone to grow their business or build their own personal brand.

You probably use social media platforms like Facebook, blogging, Twitter, Instagram, Pinterest, Google+ and others. And you have probably picked up many tips and strategies which you can share with others for profit. Why not turn your love of social media, and experience on the Internet into a business opportunity.

Many businesses and older people just don't understand the benefits of using these tools to grow their businesses. You can educate these people, show them how to utilize social networks to build their business and charge a fee to do it.

This could involve training, planning their business' social media strategy and even taking over this role for the company. There are many opportunities in this hot market.

Your first step should be to research everything you can find on social media marketing, and the best social media tools and platforms. Learn how to create social media plans for prospective clients.

In order to build credibility as a social media "expert" you need to show results. If you haven't already, sign up for every social media platform that is garnering attention. These include Facebook, Twitter, LinkedIn, and Pinterest - but consider starting a blog, posting on YouTube, and others.

Start sharing valuable information and focus on building a following. Follow experts and interesting people on Twitter. Setup a Facebook page for your business. Make a habit of sharing content across all of your social media accounts, this way you will build your presence across multiple platforms.

Investigate tools like Hootsuite and Buffer to help you manage your social media strategies.

Show potential clients that you can help their business grow through social media. Offer to not only develop their social media strategy but to run their campaigns.

Focus on results and reach, and clearly show the benefits for the company or brand.

Visit these websites for more information, tips and ideas:

http://windmillnetworking.com/2010/11/26/how-to-start-a-social-media-consulting-business
www.entrepreneur.com/article/222837
www.entrepreneur.com/article/218160

CHAPTER NINETEEN

House Cleaning Business

Society continues to change, people are busier, and in many families both parents work full-time. With our hectic lifestyles, people want to enjoy their free time to relax, spend with family or take part in other activities. But housework and cleaning still need to get done.

Many people require house cleaning services on a regular basis - whether it be weekly, bi-weekly or even monthly.

This presents an opportunity. This type of business can be started with very little cost. Cleaning supplies (many clients provide their own cleaning supplies) and some advertising are all that are required. Although this business is heavily driven by word-of-mouth, in the beginning some classified advertising, flyers and other low cost methods can help drum up business.

Because the job is labor intensive, and will require driving to multiple locations, scheduling and time management are important and a vehicle will most likely be required.

Of course, it is important that you know how to clean properly and thoroughly, but chances are you have plenty of experience.

Because house cleaning often takes place while the owners are away, trust is a big part of this type of business. Being professional (not snooping or stealing) is obviously an important part of being successful in this industry. In some cases, you may need to be "bonded" and insured before clients will work with you.

Before you start promoting your business, determine what wage you will charge, for example $20 per hour. Make sure your wage is both priced well for the market and worthwhile for you personally.

Don't be surprised if you find yourself with too many clients, and too little time! This business service is in high demand, and you if you do good work, you may have no problem at all finding clients!

Visit these websites for more information, tips and ideas:

www.entrepreneur.com/article/41426
www.wikihow.com/Start-a-House-Cleaning-Business
www.homebiztools.com/ideas/residential_cleaning.htm

CHAPTER TWENTY

Gift Basket Business

Gift baskets are a booming business because they are the perfect gift for many occasions. Whether it is a gift of congratulations, for a friend recovering in hospital, for a baby shower, or just something different and unique - gift baskets are a popular gift.

Your baskets could include candy, baking, bath items, gourmet food, and just about anything else. You can offer specialized baskets such as chocolate lovers or office themed baskets too.

Use your creativity to make your baskets the perfect gift, or allow your clients to provide their own ideas!

Decide early on whether or not you will service your local area only, or if you will consider shipping baskets to customers across the country. Will you offer free local delivery, or will customers pick up the baskets from your home or retail location?

You could easily run your gift basket business from your home, even on a part-time basis.

Build your business using local marketing and word-of-mouth. Utilize a website to showcase your work. Consider joining image sharing sites like Pinterest to promote your creations.

You might also consider selling your gift baskets to other retailers at a discount. Businesses such as flower shops, bakeries, or candy shops may be interested in your basket designs which they can add their own products to and up sell to their customers.

Visit these websites for more information, tips and ideas:

www.entrepreneur.com/article/37926-1
www.powerhomebiz.com/vol100/giftbasket.htm
www.giftbasketbusiness.com/faqbasics.htm

CHAPTER TWENTY-ONE

Affiliate Marketing

Affiliate marketing has been around for years. Affiliate marketing on the Internet was made popular by Amazon.com and other online retailers who pay a commission every time an affiliate sends traffic to their site, and a purchase is made.

There are still many good affiliate programs available online, and one strategy has always been to create a website or blog focused on a particular niche area, create lots of content on the topic to drive search engine traffic to the site, and then plaster the site with affiliate ads.

Online advertising has evolved since then to include programs like Google Adsense which displays appropriate ads on your website based on the content, and then you are paid by Google for the number of clicks the ads receives (pay-per-click).

Through a combination of affiliate marketing and PPC type programs, it is still possible to bring in revenue from your website. But the secret is to promote relevant products and services to your own loyal following. Your email list is much more powerful at converting sales, than visitors to your website.

It is important to build your email list by asking readers and customers to sign up to receive information from you.

The growth of social media has also created another opportunity for affiliate marketers, but it is not nearly as effective as email marketing.

Typically there are several factors necessary to make significant revenue through affiliate programs. These include large volumes of traffic to your website or blog, a growing email list, and a lot of social media followers. It can be much easier to grow a large following on Twitter or Facebook than subscribers to your blog.

Promoting affiliate products to these channels can be very effective, provided the products are relevant to your niche, high quality and the sales copy is convincing.

It is important to remember that you have built a trusting relationship with your readers and followers - therefore offers should only be sent for products you truly do believe in. Your readers will appreciate that you are sending them useful information and tools to help them.

There are a number of excellent affiliate networks and programs on the Internet. According to The Online Advertising Blue Book (http://mthink.com/affiliate), the top five affiliate networks are Linkshare (www.linkshare.com), Commission Junction (www.cj.com), Amazon.com (https://affiliate-program.amazon.com), ClickBank (www.clickbank.com) and ShareASale (www.shareasale.com). I suggest you check out all of these programs to see if they are a good fit for you.

Each of the affiliate networks has numerous programs within it, from different retailers - including top names like Walmart, AT&T, and Barnes & Noble.

I have personally purchased information products and WordPress plugins via ShareASale and JVZoo.com and have been very pleased. In fact, I was so impressed by the products I have used as a consumer/business owner, that I became an affiliate for the sites myself.

Affiliate marketing is alive and well, and can create a significant stream of income for you if you have the ability to reach targeted audiences via your websites, blogs, email lists and even social media.

For more information, explore the following links:

www.theprofitshare.com/5-tips-for-starting-an-affiliate-marketing-business
www.problogger.net/archives/2009/07/07/what-is-affiliate-marketing
www.seodesignsolutions.com/blog/how-to-reference-material/how-to-start-an-online-affiliate-business

CHAPTER TWENTY-TWO

Internet Retailer

Online sales continue to grow each year. Popular online retailers like Amazon.com and Overstock.com have billions of dollars in sales annually. Every major brand and retailer has an online presence and the majority of them sell directly online as well.

The secret to starting your own online retail business is to focus on a niche market. Perhaps you make your own products such as woodworking, crafts or other unique items. Maybe you collect comic books, Star Wars figurines or trading cards. You can sell these products online on your own website, eBay or utilize other e-commerce platforms like Amazon or Yahoo web stores or even Shopify, a very popular platform.

If you are reselling products, you will want to ensure that you have reliable suppliers, and enough space to store inventory. It is next to impossible to compete with larger, established e-commerce sites for many reasons. The secret is to sell products that very few others are selling.

The name of your online store will be important. It should be easy to remember and typically should reflect what you are selling, or some characteristic of your business.

Choose carefully and purchase the domain name right away. In most cases, the .com extension is the universally accepted and most appealing domain name extension. Choosing a domain with a country extension such as .ca for Canada is acceptable in many cases, but may not be ideal.

When developing your marketing and advertising strategies, focus on your target market. How can you best reach these buyers?

This might involve advertising on Facebook, specialized or local websites, doing a combination of print and web marketing, or using traditional channels like TV and radio. It will depend on your business.

Whatever the method, the idea is to drive traffic to your site and convert this traffic into sales.

Other considerations are physical space requirements (do you need to store inventory?), staffing (can you run this business yourself?), customer service, etc.

There are plenty of books and websites with valuable insight into selling online. As with any new business, you should do your research to see if starting an online store is something you could be successful with.

Drafting a business plan could help flesh out your idea even more, and forecast the kinds of costs involved in such a project. As mentioned earlier, you may wish to start by utilizing eBay and other low-cost platforms or webstores before spending any money developing your own e-commerce website. Think of it as a test to see if there truly is a market for your products.

Visit these websites for more information, tips and ideas:

http://inspirationfeed.com/articles/business/10-essential-tips-for-starting-an-online-store
http://webstore.amazon.com
http://smallbusiness.yahoo.com/ecommerce
www.shopify.com

CHAPTER TWENTY-THREE

Selling Online With Amazon FBA

Did you know that you can sell products on Amazon.com and have Amazon collect the payment, ship the order and even store all of your inventory?

Amazon's Fulfillment-by-Amazon program has changed the game for online sellers and created one of the greatest opportunities for people like you and me to build successful online businesses in no time at all.

Thousands of individuals are utilizing this platform to sell millions of products each and every day on Amazon.

One of the benefits of selling on Amazon is the credibility and trust that already exist with its customers. Amazon typically offers the best prices, and exceptional customer service (including return policies) – which makes selling on Amazon so easy.

For a monthly fee (currently $40) you can sign up for a professional seller account through Amazon's Seller Central (or and start your business today. Simply create your product listing(s), ship your inventory to Amazon's own warehouses, and start selling. Amazon also takes a percentage of your sales as fees for using the program.

There are numerous books and courses you can take to learn more about this business opportunity. I personally enrolled in a course myself and in July 2014 I started my business selling my own brand of products (including electronics, and houseware products) on Amazon. I was amazed at how easy the concept was and how much potential there truly is to make money using this business model.

Although almost everything I learned in the course could have been learned through trial and error, going through a complete training program allowed me to get up and running within a short period of time. Regardless of the training program, the key concepts are quite similar.

I will summarize them below:

1. Find a Product(s) – There are various techniques for finding potentially successful products to sell, but the bottom line is you want to find products that are in high demand (competitive categories), are relatively small and light weight (to keep Amazon storage fees and shipping costs low), and typically retail for between $7-40 dollars (to keep inventory costs low).

2. Source Your Product(s) – Find reliable wholesalers, distributors or manufacturers that will supply your products to you at prices that allow for a healthy profit margin. You may wish to consider utilizing www.alibaba.com to source low-cost products from China.

3. Create Your Own Brand(s) and private label your products. This technique allows you to differentiate your products from other companies and brands.

4. Create killer Amazon Listings – This step alone can help distinguish your brand from the competition. Many companies (even leading brands) sell their products on Amazon as just another sales outlet, and do little to make their product listings compelling – instead just relying on their brand name. By focusing on optimizing your title, description and product images you can have your product listing stand out from the competition!

5. Marketing and Promotion – It will be up to you to market and promote your Amazon products utilizing social media, press releases, getting blogger reviews, and even paid advertising on Facebook, Google Adwords or other methods. Strong marketing efforts can drive significant traffic to your sales pages on Amazon.

6. Reviews are King – Another way that Amazon customers benefit is through product reviews. Most customers considering buying something from Amazon will read the reviews to see if the product is of good quality and meets the expectations of existing customers. This can create a huge advantage for

sellers that focus on getting reviews from their customers. Amazon allows you to follow up with customers and provide effective customer service. This can include asking for product reviews, and let's face it, the more positive reviews your product has, the easier it will be to make future sales.

7. Customer Service – Most programs teach you to focus on providing excellent customer service in order to stand apart from the competition. This may include following up on customer emails/inquiries, offering free replacement items and responding to any negative reviews quickly. Simply going out of your way to provide an excellent buying experience will help create loyal repeat customers, build your brand and increase your sales in the long run.

There are many other techniques that can be utilized to build a successful Amazon business, but at the end of the day you want to build a successful brand, offer quality products and deliver exceptional customer service.

The level of success you can reach with an Amazon business is almost limitless with the right products, branding and ratings.

Many Amazon entrepreneurs start small and re-invest profits in their business – allowing them to invest more in product inventory and promotion.

While I have just scratched the surface of building a successful business on Amazon, I encourage you to learn more about this opportunity and see what is possible for yourself.

Below is a list of resources for further information:

http://services.amazon.com/content/fulfillment-by-amazon.htm
http://lifehacker.com/5887412/how-to-sell-your-excess-crap-for-cash-in-just-a-few-hours-with-amazons-fulfillment-program
http://provenamazoncourse.com/
www.amazing.com

CHAPTER TWENTY-FOUR

eBook/Info-Product Author

The Internet and proliferation of digital devices has changed the way people access information, and even read books and magazines. Digital versions of print books are often less expensive and more convenient to access and purchase.

While it took many years to fully catch on, with the success of the Amazon Kindle, Barnes & Noble Nook e-reader, Apple iPad and other tablets, the eBook industry is now growing at a remarkable rate.

You might have heard the term, "everyone has a book in them." It may be true that we all have potential novels in us, but the chances of writing a successful novel are very remote. It takes great imagination and writing talent to be a successful novelist. However, self-publishing is making it possible for anyone to publish their own books.

The real opportunity is in the non-fiction book genre addressing people's need for accurate, concise and valuable information. The self-help and information product market has existed for many, many years - but marketplaces like Amazon.com, Nook, iBooks and others are making it easier for buyers to find eBooks on every subject you can imagine.

Amazon.com alone has almost 200 million active customers purchasing books, eBooks, electronics and more every single day.

Selling eBooks on Amazon is like putting your sales on autopilot. If you write an eBook that provides value for a reader, by answering the questions they have about a topic, teaching them how to achieve success, or fulfilling a need that they have - then your book will be successful.

Of course, success is a subjective term, but it is quite possible to sell hundreds of books per month with very little effort (after writing, creating and uploading the book) once your book is available for sale on one or all of these marketplaces.

There are two approaches to being a successful eBook author, in my opinion. You can write eBooks about topics that you have experience or expertise in - where you want to share your knowledge. Or, you can research niche topics which sell the best and write eBooks on these topics (purely to make a profit).

However you come up with your topics, your goal will be to produce a well written, well researched "how-to" guide that satisfies the reader's interests and teaches them what they need to know about a topic.

Four areas of high interest for eBooks include weight loss, cooking, relationships and self-help. Self-help could include a wide variety of topics such as how to make money, how to be successful, and generally how to improve yourself in some specific area. Visit the Amazon.com Kindle Store to get an idea of all of the categories of eBooks available for purchase.

Your first step will be to figure out what topic you will write about. As I mentioned earlier, if you have experiences to share or expertise in a particular topic, then this is a logical starting point. Taking the other approach, you could research niche topics to determine what you will write about.

After you decide, you will want to develop an outline, to figure out what aspects of the topic you will focus on. Break it down into chapters and ensure it flows well. Next you will most likely need to do some research on the topic, or you may decide to start writing to get your own thoughts and knowledge on the page first.

I have read many books on the subject of writing and selling eBooks, and information products. In fact there are numerous Kindle eBooks on the subject - including How to Write a Book in 7 Days and many others.

Once the book is completed, reviewed and edited, you must format it correctly (which can be tricky) and convert it to an eBook format (.epub for KOBO, NOOK, and iBooks or .mobi for Amazon Kindle). Then upload the file to Amazon and/or other platforms for sale.

If you don't feel confident doing the formatting and conversion yourself, you can find individuals, virtual assistants and even eBook publishers that will do this for you for a fee (anywhere from $50 - $150). Search for these services online, but make sure to check their portfolio of previous clients.

I have been involved in the eBook industry since early 2012. My focus is on small business - including this book. I write about how to start a business, social media marketing and other small business topics. This is where my education, experience and skill set is strongest, and I always try to share useful tips, advice and strategies for success.

There are many tips I could offer about writing and selling eBooks that I have learned myself. One of the most important tips is to always have a high-quality cover for your book. It amazes me how many eBooks have cheap looking, low-quality covers. Selling your eBook online is like having a traditional book on a shelf at your local book store. The book cover is typically what draws someone to the book in the first place, and it is the same online.

Make sure that your eBooks have professional looking covers - whether you make them yourself or you have a graphic designer create them. This is one of the most important things you can do to ensure your success. Remember, you want people to find your book and purchase it online - from that point, it is the content that will determine whether the customer will be pleased or not with their purchase.

Self-published eBooks typically are priced between $0.99 and $9.99, with the majority between $0.99 and $3.99. The higher the price, the more challenging it will be to compete with books from traditional publishers or established authors.

How much can you expect to make by selling eBooks? Every platform is different, but Amazon.com pays 35% commissions on eBooks priced between $0.99 and $2.98, they increase this to 70% for eBooks priced above $2.99. Obviously it makes sense to sell your eBooks for $2.99 or more, but the eBook market is very competitive and your book must provide enough value to justify the price, or it simply won't sell.

With just one or two semi-successful eBooks, you might expect to sell between 100-300 eBooks per month. Depending on the sale price, your monthly income in this scenario could be anywhere from $35 - $600! Not bad for a part-time business venture. Of course the more eBooks you publish and the more successful each one is, the more money you will bring in. There are many examples of full-time eBook authors - perhaps you will be one of them!

EBook marketing is an entire topic on its own, but I can tell you that most authors utilize social media to promote their eBooks. Depending on the topic, you might promote your eBooks on Twitter, Facebook, LinkedIn and other eBook promotion websites. Facebook in particular has numerous groups where you can promote your books.

You might also decide to use traditional marketing such as press releases, flyers, post cards and advertising. In most cases, however, if you are selling your eBook for just a few dollars, it might not justify the expense of some traditional advertising - thus the typical focus on online promotion.

From my experience, Amazon.com is the most profitable platform on which to sell your books. Their Kindle Direct Publishing (KDP) program also offers some benefits to new authors. By signing up with KDP, you agree to sell your eBook exclusively on Amazon for 90 days and in exchange, you are allowed 5 free days (where you can give your book away to grow your readership), and your book will be included in the Amazon Prime program, where members can borrow one eBook per month. Amazon compensates authors of borrowed books by paying them from a monthly fund (typically $2 per borrow - sometimes much more than you earn from a sale).

Since Amazon is by far the largest and most popular marketplace for eBooks, KDP is a good option for most eBook authors. I recommend you compare the options available.

Below is a list of resources for further information:

http://theselfpublishingtoolkit.com/kdp-select-free-promo-resources
www.copyblogger.com/how-to-publish-kindle-ebook
www.kobobooks.com
https://kdp.amazon.com/help/
www.nookpress.com
www.apple.com/support/ibooksauthor/publishing

CHAPTER TWENTY-FIVE

Video Production

Video as a medium continues to grow in popularity, and has become more personal with YouTube, Vlogging (video blogging), and other video apps on smartphones. Today, the idea of making it big or gaining a lot of attention from videos is a reality.

Utilizing YouTube to promote your business is a bonafide social media strategy. But businesses are still looking to have professional videos created, to promote their business, enhance their brand and to connect with a younger generation of consumers.

Creating marketing and promotional videos and corporate training videos is a lucrative business that can be operated by one individual, even out of your home.

In order to capitalize on this opportunity, you must have video production skills, the right equipment, and of course, creativity. In this business, getting the shot is only half of the battle. The majority of the work takes place at your computer

- using popular software like Adobe Premiere or Final Cut Pro (MAC) to cut together all of the footage, insert transitions, music and voiceovers, text and other components.

A typical videographer making corporate videos will require several pieces of equipment in order to deliver a top product. These include a high quality video camera, or digital (DSLR) camera with video capabilities - such as the Canon EOS 6D, which has a high pixel resolution and excellent video quality. Additional lenses are often required as well, for added flexibility.

You may also require other equipment such as wireless microphones, lighting equipment, and shades, a high performance PC or MAC for processing the videos, and as previously mentioned, software to create your masterpiece!

This is potentially one of the more expensive businesses mentioned in this book; however, as many videographers are enthusiasts, they tend to justify the purchase of high quality equipment, as they often use it for both business and personal use.

You might expect to pay anywhere from $2,000 - $6,000 for a professional quality camera and lenses (although you may start your business with lower quality equipment). If you already have a solid PC or MAC, you may not need additional investment there; however, you will need to purchase the necessary software which can run between $300 - $1,000.

Additional lighting, microphones, tripods etc. can cost anywhere from $500 - $1,500, and maybe less if you purchase used equipment.

What can you expect to make in this business? I know individuals who run this type of business in their spare time (although it can be a big time commitment to complete each project) and charge anywhere from $2,000 - $10,000 per project - depending on the time required to obtain the footage, complete interviews etc. and then associated production time.

In this business, you can quickly recoup your equipment costs, and then the main cost is your time. It is important when bidding on a project or providing a quote to a client that you budget accurately for the time involved. Most videographers will budget based on a fixed hourly wage, which can make things easier.

Another added bonus for this type of business is that not only can your equipment be depreciated and written off as a business expense, but often times you can rent out your equipment to other videographers or filmmakers in your area.

Individuals I know have charged $500 per day to rent out their particular video cameras, and these are accepted rates you will find everywhere. Do a Google search for "rent video equipment NYC or Toronto" and you will see some of the daily and weekly rental costs for yourself.

This can be a great business to operate full-time or even part-time, especially if you have the passion for creative projects and of course, the videography and software editing skills required.

You can find a lot of information online about the best equipment to use, video production techniques, tutorials and much more. I advise you to check out YouTube and Google for more information. You might want to pick up the latest issue of VideoMaker or other magazines at your local newsstand.

Alternatively, check your local college for continuing education courses in video production. It might be the kick start you need to get into business.

For more information, check out these sites:

www.videomaker.com
http://smallbusiness.chron.com/start-own-video-production-company-4703.html
www.youtube.com/watch?v=n3qyi6Tn50w
www.videouniversity.com

Conclusion

You have now read through 25 in-demand, mostly low-cost, and profitable businesses you can start. Some of them require specific skills, experience or know-how and a few may require more than a basic investment. Determine which might be the best fit for you.

The next step is up to you. It is your time to decide which ideas you can take further. Deciding on the idea can be the hardest part – so consider which business ideas match up with your skills, experience, interests and market demand.

There are plenty of resources available to help you start a new business - from local business help offices, to books (including my own book - *Starting Your Own Business: An Entrepreneur's Guide to Starting and Growing a Small Business*) and Internet resources. I have provided links to more information on the next page, so that you can explore them further. I also advise that you go back to the business ideas that interest you the most, and explore some of the links I have listed.

So take that next step and further investigate one or more ideas, which will include research on the competition, the size of your market and the estimated costs for starting the business.

Take control of your future and build your own financial freedom. You can even start your business part-time and grow into a full-time passion.

Take that next step and start your own business today!

Resources & Information

Below are some local sources of information and data, as well as Internet links which will be very helpful as you explore the startup of your own small business:

- Local public library, college or university library
- Local economic or small business development offices
- Internet resources
- Business periodicals or trade publications
- Competitor websites, annual reports and other industry info
- Your local Chamber of Commerce

INTERNET RESOURCES

Business USA - http://business.usa.gov/
U.S. Census Bureau - www.census.gov/
U.S. Small Business Administration - www.sba.gov/
U.S. Government Bookstore - http://bookstore.gpo.gov/
Industry Canada - www.ic.gc.ca/eic/site/ic1.nsf/eng/home
Canada Business - www.canadabusiness.ca/
Statistics Canada - www.statcan.gc.ca
BizPal - www.bizpal.ca
Startup Canada – www.startupcan.ca
Small Business UK - www.smallbusiness.co.uk/

The UK Federation of Small Businesses - www.fsb.org.uk/
Startups UK - http://startups.co.uk/

MORE BUSINESS IDEAS

www.startupbizhub.com/
www.toiletpaperentrepreneur.com/recommendations/business-ideas-for-young-entrepreneurs/
www.startupchamp.com/

Other Books by Nevin M. Buconjic

Starting Your Own Business: An Entrepreneur's Guide to Starting and Growing a Small Business

www.ingramcontent.com/pod-product-compliance
Lightning Source LLC
Chambersburg PA
CBHW051727170526
45167CB00002B/838